I PROPHESY
LIFE

I PROPHESY
LIFE

31 Day
Prophetic Power Points

KENDREA S. STEWARD

I PROPHESY LIFE

For more information contact:
Kendreasteward35@gmail.com
www.faithtempleministriesint.com

ISBN: 978-1-7130-3256-4

Printed in the United States of America

DEDICATION

2 Samuel 23:2 "The Spirit of the LORD spoke by me, And His word was on my tongue."

First and foremost, I dedicate this publication to my Lord and Savior Jesus Christ. He has given me the supernatural ability and authority to write and share His message with the world. It has been a strong and recent burning desire to release a prophetic daily devotional from the heavens above. I dedicate this book to my oldest son Keyonta Whitlow who is anointed by God. The Lord personally ministered to my spirit through the book of Ezekiel chapter 37. The Spirit of the Lord commanded Prophet Ezekiel to prophesy to the dry bones and say to them they shall live. I didn't realize as the Lord was ministering to me through His word He was preparing me to prophesy to my son's dry bones as he nearly died six months later. I journaled every word the Spirit of the Lord gave me specifically concerning my son especially when He said prophesy to the dry bones and they shall live and He would gradually heal him. Unfortunately, the Spirit of the Lord did not share the details of why I would need to prophesy life to my son. Prophets don't know everything we only know what God tells us. He can't tell us everything because we can't handle everything. The presence, power of prayer, prophetic and journaling has been powerful tools used in my intimate relationship with the Lord. As I was in the hospital with my son the Lord led me to the very words I journaled as He spoke to me six months prior. It brought tears, confirmation and inexpressible inspiration to my spirit. Each day at the hospital I would anoint my son with oil and prophesy to those dry bones and praise God he lived!

Ezekiel 37:7,10 "So I prophesied as I was commanded and as I prophesied, their was a noise, and suddenly a rattling; and the bones came together, bone to bone. So I prophesied as He commanded me and breath came into them, and they lived, and stood upon their feet, an exceedingly great army."

I also dedicate this book to my daughter Victory Steward who when she was born the Spirit of the Lord said you have to have faith in order to have victory (this is how she received her name). Unfortunately, after losing my daughter before her fear tried to grip my heart but God. As He spoke over me faith rose up in me mightily. I conceived, carried and delivered my Victory! She carries a strong prophetic anointing on her life at such a young age. She started sharing messages from God right before she turned seven years old. Messages from God are powerful and truly life changing.

Most importantly, I dedicate this book to you the reader who invested time and finances in this publication. Thank you so much! You are the real MVP! I pray your spirit will be stirred up mightily, a massive fire will ignite in your heart and that you will encounter the inexpressible overpowering Glory of God! May every demonic force of distraction and discouragement be dismantled and dethroned and their cords cut and burned from the first and second heavens! No weapon formed against you shall prosper and I Prophesy Life shall be a major blessing and life changer in the name of Jesus Christ! I pray a mega release of illumination, revelation and manifestation from the heavens that will bring personal revival, reformation and transformation! May the Lord bless you over and above your expectations in the name of Jesus Christ, Amen!

INTRODUCTION

I Prophecy Life is a unique daily devotional book power packed with scriptures. For the word of God is living and powerful, and sharper than any two-edged sword, piercing even to the division of soul and spirit, and of joints and marrow, and is a discerner of the thoughts and intents of the heart. All scripture is given by inspiration of God, and is profitable for doctrine, for reproof, for correction, for instruction in righteousness. Reading, studying and meditating on the word of God brings an illumination and revelation of life and power from the heavens above.

This devotional is combined with a daily prophetic message commissioning and confirming His word over your life. In 2 Chronicles 20:20 the Bible says, "Believe in the LORD your God, and you shall be established; believe His prophets, and you shall prosper. The Lord puts power and authority in the words of His prophets. These prophetic messages are from the heart of God releasing power and authority to bring change in your heart, home, marriage, children, ministry, finances, health, vision and dreams.

It is also combined with daily prophetic power points given to be spoken as prophetic declarations in the earth. You have the power to change your life through the power of the prophetic. Death and life are in the power of the tongue, and those who love it will eat its fruit.

I Prophecy Life is simply saying I Speak Life with the power and the authority the Lord Jesus Christ has given. Your life largely reflects the fruit of your tongue. To speak life is to speak God's perspective on any issue of life. To speak death is to agree with the devil and declare negativity and defeat in your life. You can birth and build things through your words or you can banish and bury things through your words. You have been given the power and supernatural ability to create your world with your words. I am a living witness as I have spoken many things into existence.

I Prophecy Life is also filled with a daily prayer to power you up for your day. Prayer is powerful when you are connected to God the Father, Jesus the Son and the Holy Spirit. Prayer is one things that all nationalities, groups, genders and religions agree with. Prayer is the key used to unlock the heavens for doors to be opened in the earth. Prayer is simply communication with the Most High God in the third dimension of heavenly places. Prayer gives Him the permission to intervene in our matters on earth. In the beginning God created man in His own image; in the image of God He created him; male and female He created them. Then God blessed them, and God said to them, "Be fruitful and multiply; fill the earth and subdue it; have dominion over the fish of the sea, over the birds of the air, and over every living thing that moves on the earth according to the book of Genesis 1:27-28. Simply speaking God gave mankind dominion on the earth and He will not go against His word. God is not a man, that He should lie, nor a son of man, that He should repent according to the book of Numbers 23:19. Pray until something happens because prayer is more powerful than people understand. One of the most important parts of prayer is listening. Be still and sit in the presence of God and hear His voice. He desires for you to be in tune with Him to hear His small still voice. In John 10:27, 28 the Bible says, "My sheep hear my voice, and I know them, and they follow Me: And I give unto them eternal life; and they shall never perish, neither shall any man." He will give you guidance, direction, restoration, strategies, encouragement, inspiration, peace and joy in His presence. It is important to be baptized with the Holy Spirit to have the spiritual ability to hear and follow what the Spirit of the Lord is speaking. God sent the Holy Spirit to lead, guide, teach, help, comfort and etc. You have a friend who sticks closer than a brother when you are in right relationship with God.

1 Corinthians 6:19 says, "Or do you not know that your body is the temple of the Holy Spirit who is in you, whom you have from God, and you are not your own?"

You are not your own and you are not alone. Being partnered with the Holy Spirit is one of the greatest partnerships you can have on the earth.

I Prophecy Life was designed to spend your first in the presence of God. Matthew 6:33 says, "But seek ye first the kingdom of God, and his righteousness; and all these things shall be added unto you." As you read and meditate on the scripture, read the prophetic message from the heavens above, prophesy out loud with the prophetic power points, then the power of prayer should lead you into the presence to hear His voice and purpose for your life for the day. This is crucial because He can prepare you for things to come.

I *Prophesy Life* has a special prophetic life journal entry section to journal your daily revelation, words of encouragement, strategies and divine instructions released from the heavens. What you capture in your journal could be major encouragement, empowerment and inspiration for you as well as others current and in years to come.

I have freely given my first to the Lord for many, many years and the power of this daily process has been phenomenal. I have countless journals and just at the right time the Lord will lead me to an old journal and speak to me, confirm things and show me how he brought blessings to pass in my life. Daily intimacy with the Lord will give you the life you never dreamed you could have and prepare you for things to come.

I Prophecy Life is released to bring you a renewed, refueled and revived life in Christ to bring heaven down to earth each day!

DAY 1

Ezekiel 37:4, 5 NKJV "Again He said to me, "Prophesy to these bones, and say to them, "O dry bones, hear the word of the LORD! 5 Thus says the Lord GOD to these bones: "Surely I will cause breath to enter into you, and you shall live.

DRY BONES YOU SHALL LIVE

Today, I come to breathe new life into the dry and lifeless places in you. There may been times in life you felt spiritually dry, brittle and or lifeless. These struggles may have been the result of the lack of a real relationship with Me as your Lord, or maybe you walked closely with Me but you allowed sins and the cares of the world to carry you away from My presence, or perhaps you've poured out and given to the point of exhaustion and you need a fresh touch from My Spirit. No matter what the case is I AM sending My Spirit to refresh, refuel and revive you! Dry bones you shall live! I want you to invite Jesus into your heart to bring life where death invaded and fresh supernatural strength where you have been dry and weary. Ask for a new anointing and a fresh infilling of the Holy Spirit to arrest and overtake you.

1

PROPHETIC POWER POINTS

I PROPHESY the Lord is bringing me out of a place of death into new life and hope in the name of Jesus Christ

I PROPHESY the Spirit of the Lord is present to touch me, heal me and to lead me to Jesus to receive new life in the name of Jesus Christ

I PROPHESY the Lord has not left me and is well able to deliver me from anything that is trying to kill, steal or destroy me in the name of Jesus Christ

I PROPHESY I shall repent for all of my sins and walk in holiness in the name of Jesus Christ

I PROPHESY the Spirit of the Lord shall come upon me to anoint me to walk in freedom and deliverance in the name of Jesus Christ

PROPHETIC PRAYER

Heavenly Father,

I ask the Lord Jesus to come into my heart and fill me with a fresh infilling of the Holy Spirit. Holy Spirit I ask you to touch every desperate place in me. Let the power of God transform me, restore me completely and flow from me to those around me in the Mighty name of Jesus Christ, Amen!

PROPHETIC LIFE JOURNAL ENTRIES

_____

_____

_____

_____

_____

_____

_____

_____

_____

_____

_____

_____

_____

_____

_____

DAY 2

Psalm 37:4 AMP "Delight yourself in the Lord, And He will give you the desires and petitions of your heart."

BE INTERWOVEN IN ME

I created you as one of my prize possessions in the earth to be interwoven in Me. You were not created to be ordinary but as you are interwoven in Me you are nothing short of extraordinary. You were created for so much more. Dwell with Me on this day and forever more. It is my delight to spend private time with you. I enjoy your attentiveness and love being attentive to your every need. You are destined to learn My heart and my perfect will for your life as you meditate on My Word day and night. I will not fall short concerning the desires of your heart. As you hide in My Presence I simply deposit desires in your heart to be fulfilled. I AM the God of great fulfillment for My people. Be interwoven in Me and receive the blessings of your heart that I am awaiting to release upon your life.

PROPHETIC POWER POINTS

I PROPHESY as I delight myself in the Lord, He is giving me the desires of my heart in the name of Jesus Christ

I PROPHESY my prayers and petitions are in alignment with the heart of God in the name of Jesus Christ

I PROPHESY there is joy and the fullness thereof in the Presence of the Lord in the name of Jesus Christ

I PROPHESY the supplications of my heart shall not fall on deaf ears in the name of Jesus Christ

I PROPHESY I shall hide in the secret place of the Most High God and abide under the shadow of the Almighty in the name of Jesus Christ

PROPHETIC PRAYER

Heavenly Father,

I thank you for the opportunity to be interwoven in you God the Father, Jesus the Son and the Holy Spirit. I desire more of you and less of me. Bless me with greater wisdom, knowledge and understanding of the Lord Jesus Christ Your manifested word. As I sit in your holy presence I ask you to override all evil sent against me and to overtake me with precious Your Spirit Lord. I declare and decree the removal of every obstacle, hindrance and mountain that is in my way attempting to block my blessings in the name of Jesus Christ, Amen!

PROPHETIC LIFE JOURNAL ENTRIES

_____

_____

_____

_____

_____

_____

_____

_____

_____

_____

_____

_____

_____

_____

_____

_____

DAY 3

Psalm 105:19 NKJV "Until the time that his word (of prophecy regarding his brothers) came true, the word of the Lord tested and refined him."

THERE'S AN APPOINTED TIME IN THE HEAVENS

Prophet Joseph received a dream that his brothers would bow down to him. This dream was sent to Joseph twice. The dream was sent twice not only for confirmation but because it was established in the earth and God was destined to bring it to pass. Joseph was tested beyond our human comprehension until the word came to pass. It took many years for the dream to manifest but at the appointed time the heavens opened and manifested the blessing of promotion into Joseph's life. Sons and daughters when I send a life changing prophetic word through a dream, vision, audibly, or from my spokesperson there's an appointed time in the heavens for the manifestation of my glory. The enemy will throw everything he can your way to cause you to lose hope and destroy your faith but contend the dream deposited on the inside of you. Don't lose heart or allow your faith to fail. I am only allowing the word to test and refine you to build character and to prepare you for the manifestation of My greater glory in your life! Eyes have not seen and ears have not heard neither have entered into the hearts of man what I have for you! Remember, there's an appointed time in the heavens for you!

PROPHETIC POWER POINTS

I PROPHESY supernatural durability to withstand every test and trial sent to refine me in the name of Jesus Christ

I PROPHESY the spirit of frustration and failure is destroyed by the fire of God in the name of Jesus Christ

I PROPHESY every prophetic word spoken from the Spirit of God will manifest in the natural realm in the name of Jesus Christ

I PROPHESY every demonic force is being impeached and destroyed by the sword of God that is sent to kill, steal and destroy the word of God spoken over my life in the name of Jesus Christ

I PROPHESY heaven and earth will pass away but the Word of God will always remain and produce powerful blessings in my life in the name of Jesus Christ

PROPHETIC PRAYER

Heavenly Father,

I thank you and I praise you for every Spirit filled word spoken over my life from your heavenly throne. Give me the patience to persevere when I see contrary to the prophetic word. May the fruit of the word cause a supernatural shift in my life that will show forth visibility. I ask you for your wisdom to maintain and sustain everything that is being released in my care. I know the heavens are open and connecting with every word spoken from my mouth because there is death and life in the power of my tongue! May my thoughts, words and actions bring your name glory, in the heavens and earth, in the name of Jesus Christ, Amen!

Kendrea S. Steward

PROPHETIC LIFE JOURNAL ENTRIES

DAY 4

Genesis 50:20 NKJV "But as for you, you meant evil against me; but God meant it for good, in order to bring it about as it is this day, to save many people alive."

YOU ARE POSITIONED FOR PROMOTION

Good morning My chosen one! I have not over looked you the very masterpiece I created. I AM positioning you for your promotion. Prophet Joseph went through a painful process of long suffering before he reached the promise of promotion. His brothers initially tried to murder him and then decided to throw him into a ditch and sale him as a slave. As you begin your day let My Spirit intoxicate you. Take a deep breath and inhale the promise of promotion I have personally given to you. Your dreams are not for everyone's ears simply because their hearts can't handle it. Sadly, everyone is not for you because I chose you to do some amazing things in the earth. It's normal to feel rejected and neglected but I have you protected. What I position for promotion I separate and set apart for My glorious use. Every evil plot and plan set against you for your down fall is destined to work in your favor and for your good. It is meant to bring about a change in the earth and many will be saved to live life beyond their imagination. Even Prophet Joseph told his brothers with a clean heart of love and forgiveness what they did was meant for evil but God meant it for his good! Don't fret you are being positioned for promotion!

PROPHETIC POWER POINTS

I PROPHESY every curse sent against me is turning into a blessing in the name of Jesus Christ

I PROPHESY all things are working for my good because I love God and I am called according to His purpose in the name of Jesus Christ

I PROPHESY I am being positioned for my promotion and blessings shall overflow in my life in the name of Jesus Christ

I PROPHESY every diabolical assignment sent for my destruction is producing spiritual maturation and working for my good in the name of Jesus Christ

I PROPHESY every hidden and hindering spirit of anger and lack of forgiveness is paralyzed, dethroned and destroyed at the root of inception in the name of Jesus Christ

PROPHETIC PRAYER

Heavenly Father,

I ask you to cover me and everything connected to me with the blood of Jesus Christ. I declare and decree every evil plan devised against me and every word spoken curse is nullified and voided out in the in name of Jesus Christ. Remove all un-forgiveness, malice, strife, anger, bitterness, jealousy, double mindedness and pride from my heart. Let your goodness and mercy flow and follow me all the days of my life as I am positioned for promotion in the name of Jesus Christ, Amen!

PROPHETIC LIFE JOURNAL ENTRIES

_____

_____

_____

_____

_____

_____

_____

_____

_____

_____

_____

_____

_____

_____

_____

DAY 5

2 Timothy 1:7 NKJV "For God has not given us a spirit of fear, but of power and of love and of a sound mind."

BE FEARLESS IN CHRIST

I created you to be fearless when I released my power and authority unto you to walk in alignment to the frequency of the heavens. Many people secretly struggle with the spirit of fear or the feeling of danger. This torments the minds and hearts of people. You could be struggling with the fear of failure, fear of rejection, fear of success or fear of man. The spirit of fear will always try to cripple or corrupt your thinking to destroy the plans I have for you. The spirit of fear is an identity thief! Don't allow the spirit of fear to paralyze you from presenting your true self to the world. I have given you creativity and confidence! Boldness and courage! Passion and power! Life and love! You are more than a conqueror in Christ Jesus. Never allow the lies of the spirit of fear to be louder than truth from My Holy Spirit. Your faith in me was created to be bigger than fear from the enemy. No matter what life throws your way be fearless in Christ!

PROPHETIC POWER POINTS

I PROPHESY the spirit of fear will not alter nor change my mindset in the name of Jesus Christ

I PROPHESY my faith in God is bigger than any fear from the enemy in the name of Jesus Christ

I PROPHESY the spirit of fear shall not be a dream killer and my faith will be a dream fulfiller in the name of Jesus Christ

I PROPHESY my spirit, mind, body and soul functions in the perfect will of God in the name of Jesus Christ

I PROPHESY I am free from fear, frustration, stress and anxiety in the name of Jesus Christ

PROPHETIC PRAYER

Heavenly Father,

I bless Your Mighty and Magnificent name! I dismantle and dethrone the principality of fear that has crippled, paralyzed and kept the people of God bound. I cut and burn their cords from the first and second heavens in the name of Jesus Christ. I send forth the spirit of truth to demolish every lie from the enemy and his agents and cohorts. Help me to be wise as a serpent and harmless as a dove. I release a fresh spirit of courage, boldness and power over my life in the name of Jesus Christ, Amen!

PROPHETIC LIFE JOURNAL ENTRIES

DAY 6

Psalm 51:17 NKJV "The sacrifices of God are a broken spirit, a broken and contrite heart. These, O God, You will not despise."

BROKEN BUT BLESSED

Good morning Beautiful! The Son of God was broken physically and spiritually as He was nailed to the cross. It wasn't the nails that kept Him hanging on the cross, nor was it those who crucified Him. It was His obedience up to death because He was my secret weapon before I formed the heavens and the earth. Before He came to walk the earth, die a criminals death, be buried and raise from the dead He was the Sacrificial Lamb! He sacrificed His life for all mankind. You are called to pattern your life after Christ knowing you will fall short of my glory, unlike My Son. Sacrifices unto Me are broken spirits, a broken and contrite heart. I will not despise these and will wash and cleanse you. As I mend your brokenness back together again I will purify your heart. Most people don't like to be broken but if Jesus was broken then know you will experience brokenness too. If you refuse to be broken you are refusing to be blessed and used for my glory. Your brokenness will lead to a life of blessing!

PROPHETIC POWER POINTS

I PROPHESY the Lord will never leave nor forsake me in the name of Jesus Christ

I PROPHESY I am not broken beyond repair in the name of Jesus Christ

I PROPHESY God is mending every broken piece of my heart back together again in the name of Jesus Christ

I PROPHESY my Father in Heaven is the Great Repairer and He's fixing what is broken and giving me a life of blessing in the name of Jesus Christ

I PROPHESY the Spirit of the Lord is transmitting peace and joy in my life right now in the name of Jesus Christ

PROPHETIC PRAYER

Heavenly Father,

I ask you to help me draw closer unto you even when life is going well for me. Help me to come into your presence each morning before I start my day. Teach me and position me to be in your perfect will all the days of my life. Destroy the spirit of heaviness that tries to bring depression and oppression upon my life. Give me the oil of joy and the garments of praise. Let your love, compassion and comfort overflow in my heart and mind in the name of Jesus Christ, Amen!

PROPHETIC LIFE JOURNAL ENTRIES

_____

_____

_____

_____

_____

_____

_____

_____

_____

_____

_____

_____

_____

_____

DAY 7

Joshua 1:9 NKJV "Have I not command you? Be strong and of good courage; do not be afraid, nor be dismayed, for the Lord your God is with you wherever you go."

YOUR SET BACK IS A SET UP FOR SUCCESS

Although, you may not understand this season of your life, I know exactly what I AM doing. If I gave you a rubber band and told you to put two fingers in the middle of the rubber band holding it and using one finger to pull the rubber band all the way back and let it go. The rubber band would fly all the way forward! Sometimes what appears to be a set back I will use as a set up for your success! I AM using the very thing the enemy sent to kill you to propel you into a greater dimension of your destiny! You are destined to surpass the status quo! Prosperity and good success is your portion! You are entitled to the blessings of Abraham! Prosperity and success is in your spiritual DNA! Be strong and of good courage your set back is a set up for success!

PROPHETIC POWER POINTS

I PROPHESY every diabolical disappointment sent to destroy me is dismantled and destroyed by the fire of God in the name of Jesus Christ

I PROPHESY I take authority over my future and walk in success and prosperity in the name of Jesus Christ

I PROPHESY I walk in my divine purpose with passion and no restrictions in the name of Jesus Christ

I PROPHESY my destiny shall not be disrupted by the enemy in the name of Jesus Christ

I PROPHESY my ears are open to hear new God ideas in the name of Jesus Christ

PROPHETIC PRAYER

Heavenly Father,

I ask you to lead and guide me into complete oneness with you and your precious Holy Spirit. Release a spirit of boldness and courage like you released upon Joshua. Release warfare strategies and a mindset to conquer and win in the matchless name of Jesus Christ, Amen!

PROPHETIC LIFE JOURNAL ENTRIES

_____

_____

_____

_____

_____

_____

_____

_____

_____

_____

_____

_____

_____

_____

_____

_____

DAY 8

Philippians 3:13 NKJV "Brethren, I do not count myself to have apprehended; but one thing I do, forgetting those things which are behind and reaching forward to those things which are ahead. I press toward the goal for the prize of the upward call of God in Christ."

YOU CONQUERED YOUR PAST

Your past was never meant to define your future. The Apostle Paul had a horrendous past. He was tenacious and zealous in his pursuit of destroying Christians. He was an all star for the wrong team. However, there was an appointed time when he met the King of Glory on the road of Damascus. This blinding encounter caused an entire shift in his existence. He was converted to an all star on the right team. Nevertheless, his past did not define his future. I still used him as one of the greatest Apostles of the Lord Jesus Christ. You may not be where you want to be but there's one thing you must know. You have conquered your past! You shall no longer allow it to be a hinderance or huge obstacle in your life. I have given you a new name, future and a hope. Live and move forward toward the things which are ahead. Brighter days are in your future. Your latter shall be greater than your past! Press toward the mark of the high calling in Christ Jesus and remember you conquered your past!

PROPHETIC POWER POINTS

I PROPHESY every diabolical assignment sent to keep me focused on my past is annihilated in the name of Jesus Christ

I PROPHESY my eyes will stay focused on Jesus and He will keep me in perfect peace in the name of Jesus Christ

I PROPHESY I have not arrived but I am not where I use to be and will make it to my destiny in the name of Jesus Christ

I PROPHESY the blueprint to my destiny has been written and implemented in the name of Jesus Christ

PROPHESY no demon shall be able to resurrect my past in the name of Jesus Christ

PROPHETIC PRAYER

Heavenly Father,

I thank you and bless Your Holy name! I ask you never to allow my past mistakes to destroy the purpose and plans you have for me. May your hand of glory and blessing be upon me and keep me covered with the blood of Jesus Christ. Thank you for giving me the strength and power to continue my race. I know it's not how you start but it's how you finish. Help me to finish strong in the name of Jesus Christ, Amen!

Kendrea S. Steward

PROPHETIC LIFE JOURNAL ENTRIES

_____

_____

_____

_____

_____

_____

_____

_____

_____

_____

_____

_____

_____

_____

DAY 9

Jeremiah 33:3 NKJV "Call to Me, and I will answer you and show you great and mighty things, which you do not know."

WHEN YOU CALL I WILL ANSWER

I promised Jeremiah that if he would call unto Me, not only would I answer him, but I would reveal to him great and mighty things. I AM God of your Lord Jesus Christ, the Father of glory. I shall give unto you the spirit of wisdom and revelation in the knowledge of Him. I will reveal my secrets and mysteries unto you as you come into My presence and call on My name. I am opening your spiritual eyes so you will see beyond the surface and into the supernatural realm. I want to show you the deeper things of My kingdom. I will open your spiritual ears so you may hear what I am saying in this season beyond your home, city, state and region. You are My sheep and you know and hear My voice. The voice of a stranger you shall not follow. When you call upon My name I will always answer you just like I answered Jeremiah. I never sleep nor slumber. I encourage you to come into My presence and receive revelatory insight as I release things that would be naturally inaccessible. I will answer you in ways and show you things that will bring great astonishment to your soul.

PROPHETIC POWER POINTS

I PROPHESY the heavens are opening as I connect with God my Lord Jesus Christ in prayer and revelations are being released in the name of Jesus Christ

I PROPHESY my eyes are enlightened with understanding from the spirit of wisdom and revelation in the name of Jesus Christ

I PROPHESY I shall sit at the feet of Jesus and learn from Him each day in the name of Jesus Christ

I PROPHESY I am filled with love, peace and joy as I sit in His presence in the name of Jesus Christ

I PROPHESY greater visibility in the spiritual realm in the name of Jesus Christ

PROPHETIC PRAYER

Heavenly Father,

Thank You for Your Faithfulness in my life. Thank You for never leaving nor forsaking me when I needed You the most. I ask You to continue to shower me with Your love and be attentive to my call. Increase Your revelations in my life like never before. Speak to me and show me things I do not know in my dreams and visions. Your word says you never do anything without revealing Your secrets unto Your servants the prophets. Help me to sit in Your Presence and be diligent in waiting for Your voice in Jesus Christ name, Amen!

PROPHETIC LIFE JOURNAL ENTRIES

_____

_____

_____

_____

_____

_____

_____

_____

_____

_____

_____

_____

_____

_____

_____

_____

DAY 10

Zephaniah 3:17 NKJV "The Lord your God in your midst, the Mighty One, will save; He will rejoice over you with gladness, He will quiet you with His love, He will rejoice over you with singing."

SADNESS SHALL TURN TO GLADNESS

Rejoice in the Lord on this day! I AM worthy of your praise! I created the heavens and the earth and all things in it. I sing, shout for joy and dance over you because of the intense love I have for you. My love runs deeper and wider than the seas and oceans in all the earth. Because your finite mind could not comprehend my agape love I sent My only begotten Son Jesus Christ to demonstrate My love in the earth realm through His death, burial and resurrection. Receive My love today in a way you've never received it before. I AM releasing a new joy in your life! I AM giving you a fresh freedom and canceling every limitation sent against you from the kingdom of darkness. I AM sending My love to flow like a river in every area and aspect of your life. The spirit of heaviness is lifting off your life right now and removing the grips of oppression and depression. I AM giving you beauty for ashes. The oil of joy for the spirit of heaviness and the garments of praise. You shall walk in gladness and no longer sadness! You shall be encouraged and no longer discouraged! Rejoice!

PROPHETIC POWER POINTS

I PROPHESY I will live a life full of joy, peace and prosperity in the name of Jesus Christ

I PROPHESY I will rejoice and sing a new song unto the Lord in the name of Jesus Christ

I PROPHESY I shall rejoice unto the Lord as He has chosen me to do great exploits in the name of Jesus Christ

I PROPHESY the heavens and the earth shall respond to my praise in the name of Jesus Christ

I PROPHESY I comprehend with all saints what is the breadth and length and depth and height of the love and knowledge of God in the name of Jesus Christ

PROPHETIC PRAYER

Heavenly Father,

Thank You for providing a deeper insight for the love you have for Your children. I will rejoice in knowing you are rejoicing over me with gladness, quieting me with Your love and rejoicing over me with singing. Thank You for love and compassion toward me. Thank You for sending Jesus to save me from Your wrath, judgement and allowing me to be clothed with the robe of righteousness in Jesus Christ name, Amen!

PROPHETIC LIFE JOURNAL ENTRIES

_____

_____

_____

_____

_____

_____

_____

_____

_____

_____

_____

_____

_____

_____

DAY 11

Isaiah 42:9 NKJV "Behold, the former things have come to pass, and new things I declare; Before they spring forth I tell you of them."

I AM DOING A NEW THING

I AM doing a New thing! I AM putting New dreams in your belly! New possibilities and opportunities are coming your way! Get tuned up so you can be in tune with My Precious Holy Spirit. I am removing the old and the dead because they are no longer relevant. Your old season is stale and has expired. Don't look back as somethings are not meant to be resurrected. I AM doing a deep cleansing and removing the disappointments, hurt and pain. I AM removing the heavy burdens, chaos, situations and unfavorable circumstances. They will no longer have power over you! I AM DESTROYING yokes and BREAKING bondages! Move forward and grab ahold to the NEW blessings that I have designed to overtake you in this new season!

PROPHETIC POWER POINTS

I PROPHESY a new and fresh anointing flowing unhindered and uncompromised in the name of Jesus Christ

I PROPHESY new ideas, concepts, strategies and vision in the name of Jesus Christ

I PROPHESY the mind of Christ and new ingenious ideas in the name of Jesus Christ

I PROPHESY the power to break free from the old and move forward into the new in the name of Jesus Christ

I PROPHESY spiritual maturation as I walk in my new season of favor in the name of Jesus Christ

PROPHETIC PRAYER

Heavenly Father,

Let fresh manna fall straight from heaven! Thank you for delivering me from the old things and propelling me into my new season. I believe by faith this new season will send new blessings, favor and love overflowing in my life like never before in the name of Jesus Christ, Amen!

PROPHETIC LIFE JOURNAL ENTRIES

_____

_____

_____

_____

_____

_____

_____

_____

_____

_____

_____

_____

_____

DAY 12

Matthew 14:28, 29 "And Peter answered Him and said, "Lord, if it is You, command me to come to You on the water." 29 So He said, "Come." And when Peter had come down out of the boat, he walked on the water to go to Jesus."

COME OUT OF COMFORT WALK IN THE SUPERNATURAL

It's natural in your humanity to operate in a safe way. Safety and precaution is always good. However, it takes courage and faith to go into the unknown, to take risks and pursue what has never been done. I am convinced as a Woman of God we are called to take risk obviously with wisdom and discernment. The Bible says we shall walk by faith and not by sight. Let's not forget the just shall live by faith. When God calls you out into the unknown He is testing your obedience. Obedience is better than sacrifice and sometimes your obedience is the sacrifice. Peter and the other disciples were comfortable in the boat even in the midst of the storm. But Peter decided to break free from his place of comfort. He wanted more!! He desired the Supernatural!

He asked Jesus, if it's You command me to come walk with You on the water! Jesus said Come! Peter took the risk! He stepped out on faith to walk on water with Jesus! Although, Peter took his eyes off Jesus and began to drown he still experienced the supernatural! Today, Jesus is saying Come and experience the Supernatural!

PROPHETIC POWER POINTS

I PROPHESY the heavens to open over my life and respond to my courage, faith and obedience in the name of Jesus Christ

I PROPHESY I will get out of the boat and destroy the spirit of comfort and complacency in my life in the name of Jesus Christ

I PROPHESY I am breaking free from fear and walking by faith not by sight in the name of Jesus Christ

I PROPHESY I am set apart to set ablaze a new path for those who are stagnant in the name of Jesus Christ

I PROPHESY boldness, courage and supernatural encounters in the name of Jesus Christ

PROPHETIC PRAYER

Heavenly Father,

I thank You for supernatural abilities to do what looks impossible as I call unto You. Call me out into the deep so I can experience You in deeper ways. Let Your supernatural power overtake me in the matchless name of Jesus Christ, Amen!

PROPHETIC LIFE JOURNAL ENTRIES

_____

_____

_____

_____

_____

_____

_____

_____

_____

_____

_____

_____

_____

_____

DAY 13

John 16:13 NKJV "However, when He, the Spirit of truth, has come, He will guide you into all truth; for He will not speak on His own authority, but whatever He hears He will speak; and He will tell you things to come."

YOU ARE DESTINED TO WIN

It is very important to follow the navigation of the Holy Spirit. In humanity most people follow daily routines, emotions, family, friends or just simple tradition. It is My desire that you are sensitive to My Spirit as it is against My nature to lead you wrong. I have sent the Spirit of Truth to lead, guide and instruct you. The steps of a good man are directed and established by the Lord, and He delights in his way according to Psalm 37:23. When the disciples went back to fishing, their nets were empty. When Jesus came and told them to cast their net on the right side of the boat their results were drastically different. They could not even draw the fish because of the multitude of fish in the net. This is the outcome of obedience. Follow the leading of the Holy Spirit even when it doesn't make sense or looks unfavorable. You are destined to win! It's not what you do, it's what you do according to God's will for your life that truly matters.

PROPHETIC POWER POINTS

I PROPHESY the Spirit of Truth shall lead and guide me all the days of my life in the name of Jesus Christ

I PROPHESY I am destined to win as I walk in the perfect will of the Lord in the name of Jesus Christ

I PROPHESY I shall walk in righteousness that goes beyond deeper tradition and religion of man in the name of Jesus Christ

I PROPHESY I walk in complete and total victory in the name of Jesus Christ

I PROPHESY I was born to be a winner and champion in the name of Jesus Christ

PROPHETIC PRAYER

Heavenly Father,

I thank You for fearfully and wonderfully making me and creating me in your image. As I accepted the Son of God I thank You for access to the blessings, promises and daily benefits of Your kingdom. I dismantle and dethrone every destiny devourer and destiny thief in the name of Jesus Christ. No weapon formed against me shall prosper and the gates of hell shall not prevail against my victory. I shall walk in the purposes and promises of God everyday of my life in the name of Jesus Christ, Amen!

PROPHETIC LIFE JOURNAL ENTRIES

_____

_____

_____

_____

_____

_____

_____

_____

_____

_____

_____

_____

_____

_____

_____

_____

DAY 14

Isaiah 60:1 KJV "Arise, shine, for thy light is come, and the glory of the Lord is risen upon thee."

ARISE, SHINE & POSSESS THE GLORY OF GOD

Get up My Child and get your shine on. It's an emergency that you emerge! I am calling you out of place of obscurity into a place of visibility. I AM enlarging your territory and increasing your influence in the earth. I have called you out of darkness into My marvelous light. Every man who follows Me will have light of life. In the spiritual realm light represents life. I AM light and I give life. I AM raising you up to be light that shines in darkness. You are not called to be like the world but you are called to be the light of the world. You are the light of the world and a city that is set on a hill cannot be hidden. Your time of isolation and being hidden in plain sight is over. My light that has come upon you is opening your eyes to the treasures of My kingdom giving you revelation. My glory shall not on dwell with you but it shall rest upon you wherever you go according to My perfect will.

PROPHETIC POWER POINTS

I PROPHESY I am moving from a place of obscurity to prominence in the name of Jesus Christ

I PROPHESY I the glory of God shall change my life in the name of Jesus Christ

I PROPHESY I am living in the glory realm where miracles, signs and wonders are supernaturally normal in the name of Jesus Christ

I PROPHESY I walk in the blessings of the glory in the name of Jesus Christ

I PROPHESY the glory of God released in my life is causing me to rise, shine and putting me in a place of promotion in the name of Jesus Christ

PROPHETIC PRAYER

Heavenly Father,

I ask for a deep personal awakening and an amazing encounter in the glory realm. Let the glory of God not only dwell but rest upon my life. Pour a rich oil upon me that will cause new strategies from heaven, ingenious ideas, uncommon wisdom and ridiculous favor to come into my life. Mantle me with Your glory O Lord. Release Your glory that will bring promotion, elevation, increase, multiplication, peace and prosperity in the name of Jesus Christ, Amen!

Kendrea S. Steward

PROPHETIC LIFE JOURNAL ENTRIES

_____

_____

_____

_____

_____

_____

_____

_____

_____

_____

_____

_____

_____

Psalm 1:3 "He shall be like a tree planted by rivers of water, that brings forth its fruit in its season, whose leaf also shall not wither; and whatever he does shall prosper."

YOU ARE ESTABLISHED IN THE EARTH

You were not created to be like a fly by night business, singer or actress. You are not a one hit wonder. You are established in the earth like a tree planted by rivers of water which is the Word of God. The Word of God washes and cleanses! The Word of God gives direction and guidance! The Word of God is truth! You are established in the earth as My instrument! You shall bring forth fruit in due season! Your due season shall come so keep reading, study, praying and doing the work of the Lord! Your leaves shall not wither and die because you are connected to the Vine and the Vinedresser! Whatever you do it shall prosper when you are in complete communion and fellowship with Me!

PROPHETIC POWER POINTS

I PROPHESY I shall meditate on the Word of God day and night in the name of Jesus Christ

I PROPHESY I am established in the earth to do great things for and in Christ in the name of Jesus Christ

I PROPHESY I am blessed because I do not walk in the counsel of the ungodly in the name of Jesus Christ

I PROPHESY I walk in growth and maturity in Christ in the name of Jesus Christ

I PROPHESY I pray without ceasing to accomplish the perfect plans of God in the earth in the name of Jesus Christ

PROPHETIC PRAYER

Heavenly Father,

I thank You and praise You for Your faithfulness! Teach me Your ways and help me to be established in the earth as Your end time warrior. As I plant and water others Lord I ask You to give the increase. Increase in me so that I will continue to grow in Christ and teach others the deity of Christ in the name of Jesus Christ, Amen!

PROPHETIC LIFE JOURNAL ENTRIES

DAY 16

Psalm 110:1 NKJV "The LORD said to my Lord, Sit at My right hand, Till I make Your enemies Your footstool."

USE YOUR ENEMIES AS ELEVATORS

Rise up! Be alert and sober minded My child. Your enemy the devil prowls around like a roaring lion looking for someone to devour. Be wise as a serpent and harmless as a dove. I warned you in My word you would be persecuted and reviled for righteousness sake. The persecution could come from a family member, close friend, co-worker and or church member. The enemy will use those who are close to ensure the attack is effective. Your weapons of warfare are not carnal but mighty in the pulling down of strongholds, casting down imaginations and everything that exalts itself against the knowledge of God. Blessings are produced and released when you are persecuted for the sake of the Gospel. I AM a God of miracles, signs and wonders. I have given you the undefeated and ultimate victory through the life of my precious Son Jesus Christ. When your enemies are sent to devour you I have already made them a public spectacle and your footstool. I only allow them to come because a footstool is symbolic to your future elevation. When your enemies come elevation comes shortly after! Be encouraged your labor and endurance is not in vain! Use your enemies as elevators!

PROPHETIC POWER POINTS

I PROPHESY the Lord Almighty will make my enemies my footstool in the name of Jesus Christ

I PROPHESY I am wise as a serpent and harmless as a dove in the name of Jesus Christ

I PROPHESY the angels from heaven are heeding to the Word of God on my behalf in the name of Jesus Christ

I PROPHESY the Lord is my Rock and my Salvation in the name of Jesus Christ

I PROPHESY when the enemy comes against me he has to flee seven different ways in the name of Jesus Christ

PROPHETIC PRAYER

Heavenly Father,

I thank You and praise You for divine protection and the power of the cross! Thank You for giving me the power to declare victory over my life through the blood of Jesus Christ. No weapon formed against me shall prosper and every tongue that rises against me in judgement shall be condemned in the name of Jesus Christ, Amen!

Kendrea S. Steward

PROPHETIC LIFE JOURNAL ENTRIES

_____

_____

_____

_____

_____

_____

_____

_____

_____

_____

_____

_____

_____

DAY 17

John 15:11 NKJV "These things I have spoken to you, that My joy May remain in you, and that your joy may be full."

YOUR JOY SHALL REMAIN

The fullness of joy is a divine quality of character that is possessed and only given by the Spirit of God. I can point the way to such joy. It is my desire to lead you to be filled with unspeakable joy. As you come into My presence there is joy and the fullness thereof. I want to shower you with the fullness of My love, good pleasure and true happiness. Every void sent from the hand of the enemy to cause you to be incomplete, insufficient and deficient shall be filled with my peace, love and inexpressible glory of joy! Your joy shall remain!

PROPHETIC POWER POINTS

I PROPHESY I am overtaken by the Spirit of Joy in the name of Jesus Christ

I PROPHESY I rejoice in the Lord as I am privileged to do the will of my Father in heaven in the name of Jesus Christ

I PROPHESY every demonic and hindering spirit sent to steal my joy is dismantled and destroyed in the name of Jesus Christ

I PROPHESY supernatural joy and abundant blessings in every area of my life in the name of Jesus Christ

I PROPHESY all demonic assignments of sadness, depression, oppression and defeat are dismantled and destroyed in the name of Jesus Christ

PROPHETIC PRAYER

Heavenly Father,

I thank You and Praise You for a day filled with unlimited joy. Bless me with more of Your joy the fruit of the Holy Spirit and saturate me with the oil of joy over my life in the name of Jesus Christ, Amen!

PROPHETIC LIFE JOURNAL ENTRIES

_____

_____

_____

_____

_____

_____

_____

_____

_____

_____

_____

_____

_____

_____

_____

DAY 18

Ephesians 3:20 NKJV "Now to Him who is able to do exceedingly abundantly above all that we ask or think, according to the power that works in us"

YOU SHALL LIVE IN THE OVERFLOW

I have given you boldness and access with confidence through faith in My Son, Jesus Christ. Do not lose heart! The trials and tribulations are an intricate part of your story in which displays My glory in your life. Be strong in the Lord knowing I AM well able to do exceedingly and abundantly above all you can ask or think according to the power that works within you. The Holy Ghost Power I deposited on the inside of you. You are not alone. I sent you a Helper. I desire to manifest My glory in your life in ways that you have never dreamed. My weighty presence will crush the powers of hell and send your life into a new direction flowing with milk and honey. My glory shall bring forth transformation and redefinition. You shall go from glory to glory in Christ Jesus. Your drought and just enough season is being destroyed! You shall live in the overflow and great abundance according to My will!

PROPHETIC POWER POINTS

I PROPHESY the glory of the Lord is filling my life with an overflow of favor, increase, abundance, excellence and honor in the name of Jesus Christ

I PROPHESY every limitation in my life is being broken and destroyed by the glory of God in the name of Jesus Christ

I PROPHESY I boldness and access to the kingdom of heaven through my faith in Jesus in the name of Jesus Christ

I PROPHESY I shall walk in a dimension of glory that will shake the nations in the name of Jesus Christ

I PROPHESY I will get so lost in God that everyone I come in contact with will encounter the power of God in the name of Jesus Christ

PROPHETIC PRAYER

Heavenly Father,

I bless Your Holy name and thank You for the power of Your might. Let Your glory fill this place. Let your all consuming fire purify my heart. Give me supernatural stamina, zeal, strength and endurance knowing You are able to bless me far above what I can ask or imagine in the name of Jesus Christ, Amen!

Kendrea S. Steward

PROPHETIC LIFE JOURNAL ENTRIES

_____

_____

_____

_____

_____

_____

_____

_____

_____

_____

_____

_____

_____

DAY 19

Matthew 11:29 NKJV "Take My yoke upon you and learn from Me, for I am gentle and lowly in heart, and you will find rest for your souls."

LAY IT DOWN

Good morning, My child. I want you to lay every burden at My feet and take My yoke upon you and receive knowledge from Me. I am gentle and humble in heart. You will find rest and revitalization for your weary soul. You will gain a renewed mind and strength in Me. I AM your surge protector! I am fully equipped to refresh and recharge you! I will carry what you cannot carry to ensure your load will never weigh you down. I AM releasing a spirit of ease to come upon you to destroy the spirit of difficulty and heaviness. You will gain more understanding of my promises as you rest in Me. I will supply all of your need according to My riches and glory in Christ Jesus. Follow Me to this place of rest, peace, love, enjoyment, laughter, blessing, prosperity, unity and supernatural acquisition I have waiting for you. When you lay it down I will pick you up and take care of everything you need.

I PROPHESY I train my ear to learn from the Lord in the name of Jesus Christ

I PROPHESY a refreshing and a refueling to come upon me in the name of Jesus Christ

I PROPHESY the spirit heaviness will no longer weigh me down and is destroyed by fire in the name of Jesus Christ

I PROPHESY I receive rest and relaxation for my soul in the name of Jesus Christ

I PROPHESY I walk in humility and in the blessings of the Lord they overtake me in the name of Jesus Christ

PROPHETIC PRAYER

Heavenly Father,

I thank You and praise You for Your faithfulness in my life. Thank You for lifting every heavy burden that was sent to weigh me down and abort my mission. I cancel the assignment of every diabolical assignment in the name of Jesus Christ, Amen!

PROPHETIC LIFE JOURNAL ENTRIES

_____

_____

_____

_____

_____

_____

_____

_____

_____

_____

_____

_____

_____

_____

_____

DAY 20

Jeremiah 29:11 NIV "For I know the plans I have for you, "declares the Lord," plans to prosper you and not to harm you, plans to give you hope and a future."

MY PLANS FOR YOU ARE SECURE FOR YOU

My child, I know you have been through so much in your life and sometimes it's difficult to realize and understand the plans I have for you. The enemy does his best to dilute and blind the eyes of people from My perfect will for their lives. Every spiritual blinder and cataracts must fall off of your eyes now. You shall have keen sight in the natural and spiritual realm. You shall discover your purpose and take your position as I have released the kingly and priestly authority, power and dominion. I am calling you into divine alignment with My perfect will for your life. The plans I have for you were secured in the heavens when you were in your mother's womb. Your destiny is settled and cannot be breached or broken. For I have great things in store for you. I have mapped out a direct path that will move you closer to your destiny. The heavens will come to earth through you and you shall break records, give new hope, create new paths and be an agent of change. In this season I am propelling you into the plans I have for you.

I PROPHESY the purposes and plans of God shall prosper in the name of Jesus Christ

I PROPHESY those who are connected to my purpose shall come forth to assist me in the name of Jesus Christ

I PROPHESY the gates of hell shall not prevail against my future in the name of Jesus Christ

I PROPHESY the hope of glory resides on the inside of me in the Name of Jesus Christ

I PROPHESY I am born to prosper in all I put my hands to according to the perfect will of my Father in Heaven in the name of Jesus Christ

PROPHETIC PRAYER

Heavenly Father,

I thank You and praise You for a time such as this. Thank you for designing my destiny before the formulation of the heavens and earth. Thank you for giving me a hope and a future that is secure in the earth. Destroy every demonic force assigned against my purpose in the Mighty name of Jesus Christ, Amen!

PROPHETIC LIFE JOURNAL ENTRIES

DAY 21

Job 22:28 NKJV "You will also declare a thing, and it will be established for you; So light will shine on your ways."

USE YOUR AUTHORITY

Good morning My dear child! I have given you legislative power and authority in your mouth to declare and decree things in the invisible realm to be established in the earthly realm! As you declare a thing you will cause a Supernatural Shift in your life! Everyone connected to you will be blessed from this shift. Giants sent against you will fail and fall! Your declarations are accepted, settled and secure in Christ! HIS light of favor shall shine on your entire existence! Use your authority with your words to shape your world!

PROPHETIC POWER POINTS

I PROPHESY whatever I declare shall be established in the earth in Jesus Christ name!

I PROPHESY the powers of hell will not shut my mouth in Jesus Christ name!

I PROPHESY the Spirit of Truth shall fill my temple and give me utterance in Jesus Christ name!

I PROPHESY my tongue shall speak life and not death in Jesus Christ name!

I PROPHESY the plans for my life are secure and history breaking in the name Jesus Christ

PROPHETIC PRAYER

Heavenly Father,

You are Awesome and Amazing! Give me tongues of fire and the burning desire to declare and decree a thing so it will be established in the earth. I come into full alignment with God the Father, Jesus the Son and the Holy Spirit. I speak to my destiny and declare it shall line up with God's authentic amazing purpose and plans for me in the name of Jesus Christ, Amen!

PROPHETIC LIFE JOURNAL ENTRIES

_____

_____

_____

_____

_____

_____

_____

_____

_____

_____

_____

_____

_____

_____

DAY 22

Isaiah 40:31 NKJV "But those who wait on the Lord shall renew their strength; They shall mount up with wings like eagles, They shall run and not be weary, They shall walk and not faint."

YOU SHALL SOAR HIGHER

Do not be speedily to be your own problem solver when you're weak remember I AM strong. I have anointed you to wait on Me. As you wait on Me I am sending you a fresh anointing with a renewed strength, mindset and clarity of vision. While you wait for your next to become your now I working behind the scenes to make sure everything fall into their respectable places. I take My time on My people who are precious to Me. I am giving you wings like eagles because eagles are known to have keen sight and powerful soaring flight ability. They don't have to flap their wings using up their strength, they soar! They soar above all things that were sent to bring them down. I cancel the assignment of the low level devils in your life. When a storm comes, the storm pushes the eagle to soar higher. I AM strengthening you in the midst of the storm. It was only sent to push you higher in Me. You shall soar higher!

PROPHETIC POWER POINTS

I PROPHESY a renewed strength and higher soaring ability in the name of Jesus Christ

I PROPHESY I shall prepare while I wait for my next to become my now in the name of Jesus Christ

I PROPHESY I will not be weary in well doing and I shall reap a bountiful harvest in the name of Jesus Christ

I PROPHESY keen sight, foresight and insight in the name of Jesus Christ

I PROPHESY greater is He who is in me than he who is in the world in the name of Jesus Christ

PROPHETIC PRAYER

Heavenly Father,

I bless Your Holy and Righteous Name! Thank You for the very strength you are releasing in my life as I wait to see the manifestation of your glory. When I do nothing you always do something. Your strength is causing me to mount up with wings like eagles. Your strength is taking me higher in you. Your strength is pushing me to rise above every problem, circumstance, obstacle, barrier and mountains in my life in the name of Jesus Christ, Amen!

PROPHETIC LIFE JOURNAL ENTRIES

_____

_____

_____

_____

_____

_____

_____

_____

_____

_____

_____

_____

_____

_____

_____

Habakkuk 2:14 NKJV "For the earth will be filled with the knowledge of the glory of the LORD, as the waters cover the sea."

MY GLORY SHALL COVER YOU

I AM sending my glory to cover you, My child. It will intoxicate and dwell with you as you chase after My heart and My fragrance. It is My desire to have a heart to heart relationship with you. I want you to be into Me through the power of spiritual intimacy. Oneness with Me brings a life of holiness and holiness brings My glory. My glory will give you supernatural strength, victory and abundant blessings. Wealth and prosperity are manifested in the glory realm. Glory and honor are in My presence. The atmospheric realm of glory is around My throne. I grant you access as you dwell close to Me. When you dwell in the secret place with Me you shall abide in My shadow. Being in My shadow requires closeness to Me. Then I will give you keys to access life in the glory realm. I will conquer your enemies as I cover you with my glory. There is unlimited power when you live in the glory realm. You will see cities, states, regions and nations shaken as you go from glory to glory. The earth shall be filled with the knowledge of My glory as the waters cover the sea. My glory shall cover you in all that you do!

PROPHETIC POWER POINTS

I PROPHESY the glory of the Lord is bringing me beauty for ashes in the name of Jesus Christ

I PROPHESY the glory of God shall reveal mind blowing revelation in the name of Jesus Christ

I PROPHESY I shall cause earth shaking eruptions and deliverance as I live in the glory realm in the name of Jesus Christ

I PROPHESY as I walk in the glory of God unusual manifestations of power is being released in my life in the name of Jesus Christ

I PROPHESY the glory of God will change my entire existence and I won't even look or act the same in the name of Jesus Christ

PROPHETIC PRAYER

Heavenly Father,

I ask you to shine forth Your glory in brilliance, excellence, majesty and beauty to overcome every demonic force of shame, defeat and dishonor in the name of Jesus Christ. I am believing You O God for your manifested glory! I prophesy I shall arise and shine for my light has come and the glory of the Lord has risen upon me. Your glory shall cover me, my family, ministries, community and region like a canopy in the mighty name of Jesus Christ, Amen!

PROPHETIC LIFE JOURNAL ENTRIES

_____

_____

_____

_____

_____

_____

_____

_____

_____

_____

_____

_____

_____

DAY 24

Hebrews 11:3 NKJV "By faith we understand that the worlds were framed by the word of God, so that the things which are seen were not made of things which are visible."

FRAME YOUR LIFE WITH YOUR FAITH

I have given you the very ability through My Spirit to frame your world with your words. Your words are anointed and have power to create things that are seen from the unseen. This is the same power I used to frame the entire universe. It's apart of your spiritual DNA. I blew My very breath into your nostrils to give you an amazing life. I created you to be a person of destiny to leave your mark in the earth. Activate your faith and speak anointed words through the unfaltering resource of the Holy Spirit. The Word of God and the breath of God comes from my very mouth, the mouth of God. Frame your life with your faith.

PROPHETIC POWER POINTS

I PROPHESY I am filled with the indwelling of the Holy Spirit and my cup is running over in the name of Jesus Christ

I PROPHESY my words are filled with the power of God and I speak life and not death in the name of Jesus Christ

I PROPHESY the Word of God is powerful and alive bringing me daily inspiration in the name of Jesus Christ

I PROPHESY God is blowing his mighty and powerful breath on my situations causing a major turn around in my life in the name of Jesus Christ

I PROPHESY the Word of God is like a lamp unto my feet and a light unto my path giving me daily direction and guidance in the name of Jesus Christ

PROPHETIC PRAYER

Heavenly Father,

I bless Your Holy and Righteous Name! You are Holy and I declare holiness in my life on this day and forever more. I know by faith the worlds were framed by the Word of God. I know I frame my world by the words that I speak over my life from your powerful Word. My faith is founded in you and sustained through you and I thank You. I know that it is impossible to please you without faith. Give me a fresh wind of Your Holy Spirit in the name of Jesus Christ, Amen!

PROPHETIC LIFE JOURNAL ENTRIES

_____

_____

_____

_____

_____

_____

_____

_____

_____

_____

_____

_____

_____

_____

DAY 25

Amos 3:3 NKJV "Can two walk together, unless they are agreed?

THE POWER OF AGREEMENT

The power of agreement will serve as confirmation for right relationships. Those who value you will partner and partake in your dreams and aspirations. One of the greatest prayers Jesus prayed before He died on the cross was for all of the disciples, including you, to be unified as one as He was unified as one with Me, your Father in Heaven. I designed you to be evenly yoked with those who walk with you. Take inventory of your relationships and those who violate your dreams remove and those who cheer for you, cherish. The people who rejected and neglected you were led away because the power of agreement was lacking and they secretly awaited for your failure. I am sending the right people and putting you in right relationships with those who will help you excel beyond your natural limitations. I will send those who truly walk with Me. You will know them by their love and your spiritual DNA will be the same as theirs. You will not have to agree to disagree because the power of agreement and unity will be evident!

PROPHETIC POWER POINTS

I PROPHESY I have keen discernment concerning my relationships in the name of Jesus Christ

I PROPHESY my relationships are flourishing in the name of Jesus Christ

I PROPHESY I walk in unity and perfect peace in my God ordained and maintained relationships in the name of Jesus Christ

I PROPHESY the cords of ungodly covenants and meaningless relationships are being broken and destroyed right now in the name of Jesus Christ

I PROPHESY I am unified as one with God the Father, Jesus the Son and the Holy Spirit in the name of Jesus Christ

PROPHETIC PRAYER

Heavenly Father,

I thank you and praise you for your unmerited favor! I ask you to send the right people at the right time to cross my path to push me into a greater realm of my purpose. Sever every ungodly spiritual soul tie and destroy the connection I have with every person sent from the evil one to cause me to be distracted, dismayed and depressed in the name of Jesus Christ, Amen!

PROPHETIC LIFE JOURNAL ENTRIES

DAY 26

Isaiah 55:11 NKJV "So shall My word be that goes forth from My mouth; it shall not return to Me void, But it shall accomplish what I please, and it shall prosper in the thing for which I sent it."

SPEAK THE WORD AND SEE GOD MOVE

It's time for you to open your mouth and begin to bombard heaven with the Word of God through the power of prayer. I AM attentive to the prayers of the righteous and the heavens are open ready to release blessings. Prayer will produce more power in your life. I have given you the power and authority to destroy every demonic force that tries to stop you from reading, speaking and praying My word. May your spirit be Awakened to confess the word of God over your life daily. The Word of God is alive and powerful it will never return to Me void. I have given you the power to fight spiritual wars with my word. The word of God is a double edged sword sharper than any other weapon in the heavens or the earth. My word will go out to accomplish the assignment I sent it to accomplish. Speak the Word and see Me move!

I PROPHESY every Word and promise spoken prophetically over my life from the heart of God shall manifest in the name of Jesus Christ

I PROPHESY the Word of God brings life and each scripture will produce what it is set to produce in the name of Jesus Christ

I PROPHESY an increase of revelation from the Word of God in my life in the name of Jesus Christ

I PROPHESY the Lord is releasing and revealing the ability to understand His hidden wisdom in my life in the name of Jesus Christ

I PROPHESY the Lord Jesus is revealing the Word of Truth unto me in the name of Jesus Christ

PROPHETIC PRAYER

Heavenly Father,

Lord I thank you and praise you for your authentic Word of Truth. I ask you to increase and reign down your illumination and revelation unto me as I read and study your word. I pray you will release a rhema word, a right now word unto me. Give me wisdom, knowledge and understanding of the mysteries of your word. Your word is like a treasure box filled with countless and priceless treasures. Give me the keys I need to understand the treasures from the treasure box and give me a greater hunger and thirst for you and your word as I continue my journey with you. Thank You for every word spoken over my life because I know your word is truth and will be fulfilled in the name of Jesus Christ, Amen!

PROPHETIC LIFE JOURNAL ENTRIES

_____

_____

_____

_____

_____

_____

_____

_____

_____

_____

_____

_____

_____

DAY 27

Proverbs 10:22 NKJV "The blessing of the Lord makes one rich and He adds not sorrow with it."

YOU SHALL LIVE A LIFE OF BLESSING

You can find yourself working hard to accumulate wealth because it does not discriminate. You can also inherit wealth through the loss of a loved one or be next in line for the family business. You can have the big house, fancy cars and millions of dollars in the bank but only I can give you a Life of Blessing. Blessings that will not come with the sorrow of death, long hours and or compromise. I desire for you to have the best and live in total and complete abundance lacking nothing. I created you to be the head and not the tail. The lender and not the borrower. I will go before you and make your crooked places straight. When you live for Me I will put you in position to enjoy the fruit of your labor. I created you to take dominion over the earth. Begin to declare and decree the blessings of the Lord will make you rich and add no sorrow with it. You shall live a life of blessing!

PROPHETIC POWER POINTS

I PROPHESY I am blessed and highly favored by the Lord in the name of Jesus Christ

I PROPHESY the angels from heaven are bringing me what I need and removing what I do not need in the name of Jesus Christ

I PROPHESY the blessing of the Lord makes me rich and adds no sorrow with it in the name of Jesus Christ

I PROPHESY I drink the cup of blessing as I follow Christ in the name of Jesus Christ

I PROPHESY the Lord has granted me a life of blessing and favor in the name of Jesus Christ

PROPHETIC PRAYER

Heavenly Father,

I magnify Your Holy and Majestic name today! You are the Author and the Finisher of my faith. Remove and destroy all plots, plans, traps, snares, attacks and assignments from the enemy and his demons that is set to block my blessings in the Matchless name of Jesus Christ, Amen!

PROPHETIC LIFE JOURNAL ENTRIES

DAY 28

1 Corinthians 15:57 NKJV "But thanks be to God, who gives us the victory through our Lord Jesus Christ."

IT'S A FIXED FIGHT! WALK IN VICTORY!

When boxers train for a big fight they learn the strategies of their opponent. One of the most important fights when strategizing is how to knock the opponent out to receive the victory in the ring. I wanted to make sure you would win the ultimate fight of life in Christ and to ensure the victory, I sent My only begotten Son to die on the cross at Calvary! As My Son carried His cross in the earth He later died a criminal's death. Because He continued His race and completed His journey and fulfilled his purpose you have the victory! The fight is fixed! You win in Christ! Take a few moments to acknowledge Jesus Christ as your Lord and Savior and thank Him for His goodness, grace and mercy! If you have not had the opportunity to receive Christ you have the opportunity to do so now. Open up your heart and welcome the Lord Jesus Christ in and say the prayer below.

PROPHETIC POWER POINTS

I PROPHESY the fight is fixed and I walk in total and complete victory in the name of Jesus Christ

I PROPHESY the Spirit of breakthrough and victory is on my life in the name of Jesus Christ

I PROPHESY the gates of hell shall not prevail against the victory that was already won in the name of Jesus Christ

I PROPHESY anything or anyone sent to derail me from the victory shall boomerang back to the pits of hell where they belong in the name of Jesus Christ

I PROPHESY I have the power of victory in thinking, speaking, praying and actions in the name of Jesus Christ

PROPHETIC PRAYER

Heavenly Father,

I open my heart and accept Jesus Christ as my Lord and Savior Who brings forgiveness for my sins. I confess with my mouth the Lord Jesus and I believe in my heart that God raised Jesus from the dead and I am saved. Thank You for the beautiful gift of salvation and lead me to a Bible teaching, preaching healing and deliverance church so I can learn all about Jesus in the name of Jesus Christ, Amen!

PROPHETIC LIFE JOURNAL ENTRIES

DAY 29

Joel 2:28 NKJV And it shall come to pass afterward That I will pour out My Spirit on all flesh; Your sons and your daughters shall prophesy, Your old men shall dream dreams, Your young men shall see visions.

THE OIL OF THE PROPHETIC PIONEER SHALL FLOW

In the last days I AM releasing an outpouring of My Spirit in the earth realm upon My people. I will not discriminate between young and old or male and female. I AM raising up a modern day generation of Esthers, Samuels, Isaiahs, Jeremiahs, Deborahs, Paul's and Peters who will ablaze new paths, build and let their voices resound in the earth like a trumpet. Those who will not settle for mediocre but will walk boldly with courage slaying every demonic force that exalts itself against the kingdom of God. The oil of the Prophetic Pioneer in you shall flow!

I PROPHESY the Holy Spirit shall be my coach, guide and helper in the name of Jesus Christ

I PROPHESY I shall build and birth supernatural vision that will cause a shift in the earth in the name of Jesus Christ

I PROPHESY every illegal cycle in the Kingdom of God shall be broken, severed, burned and destroyed in the name of Jesus Christ

I PROPHESY every satanic window open with counterfeit blessings shall be closed and destroyed with the fire of God in the name of Jesus Christ

I PROPHESY the light of God's glory shall shine brighter in my life as I build and speak to the nations in the name of Jesus Christ

PROPHETIC PRAYER

Heavenly Father,

I know You created me not only be a change agent but to change history by sharing His Story the life of Christ. Bless me to walk in Your supernatural power, miracles, signs and wonders. Keep pouring Your oil on me to demonstrate Your glory wherever I go in the name of Jesus Christ, Amen!

PROPHETIC LIFE JOURNAL ENTRIES

_____

_____

_____

_____

_____

_____

_____

_____

_____

_____

_____

_____

_____

_____

DAY 30

James 1:17 NKJV "Every good gift and every perfect gift is from above, and comes down from the Father of lights, with whom there is no variation or shadow of turning."

ABOVE ALL YOU'RE A GIFT

Open your eyes to see the beauty I've deposited on the inside of you. I created and designed you to bear my image. I chose you to be one of My greatest earthen treasures with a richness that cannot be compared to silver or gold. I equipped you with gifts and talents perfected from heaven when My Spirit was deposited in you. You are my masterpiece specifically made with your own special identity and DNA. You are not a carbon copy of anyone you are the authentic original. I created you good and perfect and above all you're a gift to Me and to the world.

PROPHETIC POWER POINTS

I PROPHESY I have amazing treasure on the inside of me to share with the world in the name of Jesus Christ

I PROPHESY I am a special instrument and secret weapon of the Lord in the name of Jesus Christ

I PROPHESY I will create and launch what God created me to implement in the earth

I PROPHESY I will not settle for less I will walk in the blessings of Abraham in the name of Jesus Christ

I PROPHESY my mind is filled with the righteousness of God, strategies and a God ideas in the name of Jesus Christ

PROPHETIC PRAYER

Heavenly Father,

Help me to comprehend and understand You created me good and perfect as a gift from Your heavenly hands to the earth. Anoint my eyes to see from your perspective and with flames of fire. Order every step that I take so the seeds you deposited in me will give you a bountiful harvest in the name of Jesus Christ, Amen!

Kendrea S. Steward

PROPHETIC LIFE JOURNAL ENTRIES

_____

_____

_____

_____

_____

_____

_____

_____

_____

_____

_____

_____

_____

DAY 31

John 10:10 NKJV "The thief does not come except to steal, and to kill, and to destroy. I {Jesus} have come that they may have life, and that they may have it more abundantly."

I PROPHESY LIFE MORE ABUNDANTLY

My child, know that I am going to manifest my glory in a very unique way in your life. The enemy has sent many vicious attacks to destroy you and everything about you because he comes to steal, kill and destroy. A robber will only break into a home if the robber knows there is something valuable in the home. I designed and created you more valuable than rubies, diamonds, silver and gold. There is no price tag that would be sufficient for the value I placed inside of you. You will live a life of abundance, resourcefulness and prosperity. I have these things waiting for you as you travel the path of righteousness. I will give you a greater clarity and insight into My promises. I have deposited seeds of greatness on the inside of you. I am giving you wisdom well beyond your years. You will understand things that didn't make sense. I am releasing divine strategies, family unity and harmony, increase, favor and the glory of God. When the enemy comes in like a flood I will raise up a standard against him. I cancel the assignment of barrenness and release a spirit of fruitfulness and abundance upon your life. You shall overflow with life-giving and life-changing blessings.

I PROPHESY my life is transforming into an amazing life as it was designed to be in the name of Jesus Christ

I PROPHESY I release the sword of the Lord against the powers of hell assigned against my destiny in the name of Jesus Christ

I PROPHESY every wicked and satanic plot and plan against me is destroyed by the fire of God in the name of Jesus Christ

I PROPHESY I walk in abundant grace, love, tender mercies and favor in the name of Jesus Christ

I PROPHESY I shall live my best life more abundantly in the name of Jesus Christ

PROPHETIC PRAYER

Heavenly Father,

I come to you through the blood of Jesus Christ. I ask you to cover me and everyone connected to me. Anoint me with new and fresh oil and let my cup runneth over. Fill me up with your precious Holy Spirit and lead and guide me all the days of my life. Open my eyes to see the fullness of the life you have in store for me. I prophesy life and life more abundantly. I prophesy every demonic and satanic assignment, operation, seeding, work, plan, plot, activity, trap, wile and snare is bound and blocked from every area of my life. All curses, hexes, vexes, bewitchments and judgements of witches and warlocks and all acts of evil are cursed to the root. I prophesy bountiful blessings, open doors, garments of praise and prayer, the oil of joy, beauty for ashes, healing, deliverance, vision, eagle eyes, the mind of Christ, unspeakable joy, peace and love in the name of Jesus Christ, Amen!

PROPHETIC LIFE JOURNAL ENTRIES

Made in the USA
Lexington, KY
01 December 2019